Glad Wilderness

Geraldine Cannon

Plain View Press
P. O. 42255
Austin, TX 78704

plainviewpress.net
sb@plainviewpress.net
1-512-441-2452

Copyright Geraldine Cannon Becker, 2008. All rights reserved.
ISBN: 978-1-891386-45-9
Library of Congress Number: 2008928269

Cover Art: "Blue Ridge Parkway Overlook," @ Sheldon Heath.
www.SheldonHeath.com

Acknowledgment is made to the following magazines and journals for the publication of my work:

Nebo: A Literary Journal: "Sound Sense," Spring 1998; *Riverwind*: "Whisper Will," Spring 2002; *Pedestal Magazine*: "The Perfect Candidate," October 1, 2004; *Consequentiality, Vol. I, Expanding Human Consciousness*: "In the Absence of Light," "Meeting the Crone in the Early Morning," "Unmeasured Time," "Reproductions," "The Perfect Candidate," and "Irregular Trinity," February 2005; *Appalachian Pagan Association Newsletter*: "Meeting the Crone in the Early Morning," September 2005; *Southern Revival: Deep Magic for Hurricane Relief*: "Kudzu and a Question Under Moon Shine," Spring 2006 *Appalachian Women's Journal, Vol. 18, Appalachian Women's Alliance*: "Red Shoes in the Appalachian Mountains," Spring 2007, *Elsewhere: A Journal for the Literature of Place*, Vol. 1, Issue I: "Passing Phrases on Porch Construction," and "Sui Generis," Binghamton, New York, 2007.

Contents

Paulownia Speaks Of Walking With Wrinkled Feet	7
Between Lonesome Knob and Cheohee Valley	8
Kayla's Thoughts During a Stormy Ritual Separation	10
How the Conjure Woman Took Her Last Lover	11
J.T. Gets the Small-Town, Star-Struck, Wonder Why Blues	13
Mountain Storm In Flat Shoals	15
Cinderella's Prince In Salem, South Carolina	16
Red Shoes In the Appalachian Mountains	18
Unnatural Cage	19
Sound Sense	20
The Ritual Changes	21
What I Was Told About the Fire On the Mountain	23
Crazy Threads Speak	25
Telling Time	27
Seasoning	30
Montage of Days	32
Kudzu and a Question Under Moon Shine	34
Walking—My Way	35
In the Absence of Light	37
Learning To Take Positions	38
Haven	40
The First Star Out	42
Whisper Will	43
Night Echoes, and Morning	44
Breathing While He Sleeps	45
Daddy's Now Vacation	47
Falling Over Reptiles	49
Priority Mail	50
The Perfect Candidate	52
Irregular Trinity	54
When She Had Too Much To Drink At the Fall Party	55
Unmeasured Time	56
Reproductions	58
A Funny, Funny Riddle	59
Some Lines On Snow and Rising Moons	61
Vacation In the Land Down Under	63
The Residue Of Waves	65
Beginner Impromptu: Moving With Objects	67

Shaking the Tree	68
Sunday Mass—Confusion Of Hands	70
Dipped In Autumn	72
Meeting the Crone In the Early Morning	73
Glad Wilderness	74
Trio In Blue	76
Passing Phrases On Porch Construction	77
Sui Generis	78
About the Author	79

Dedication

To the one I love to walk with, my husband, Joseph Becker,
   and to our children: Jessica and Joanna—
      step by step,
          we create our own ways.
To all who wonder as they wander, and are well met along the way.

Paulownia Speaks Of Walking With Wrinkled Feet

The spring your friend, Melas, speaks of,
where waters flow spreading the petals
of most cherished flowers, is far from us.

We share the winter looking to the sky
for more than the sun, looking through
leafless branches with the careful gaze
of children—almost too grown to believe
the Makers ever gave our people wings.

We've looked over each other's shoulders,
watched each other falter, and shared
the bitter centers of fruits picked too early.
We've stumbled into soft brown apples
and scattered hard brown seeds.

His spring reminds me of fountains
our people have gone searching for—
never to return—perhaps, never to find.
Rocks have scrubbed the wander dust
from our soles. We are left

with so many wrinkles . . .
if we could spread our skin out,
we could glide.

Between Lonesome Knob and Cheohee Valley

Thinking I would catch my death of cold
on Lonesome Knob, I went alone,
to prove myself worthy of the dream I'd had.

Quite suddenly, and to my surprise, I found
a crystal phial filled with the essential oil of orange.
I stood, just looking, until my legs grew numb
with more than cold. How could this be?
Who else had been along this path?

I was captured by its appearance
in the snow: a warm orange glow in cool crystal,
half buried in an inextricable puzzle of individual
flakes all clumped together. For a moment, I felt sad
for the loser of the phial and for myself
that I would disturb this pleasant scene.
Slowly, I knelt down, scooped the snow to one side,
and loosened the phial from its delicate position.

Then I removed my gloves, and eased the phial out.
Using both hands, I held it carefully, up to the light—
observing no flaws. I began praising the Makers
until thinking I had overstayed the cold. I prepared to leave.

Walking to Cheohee, I will ponder the meaning
of my discovery. At Cheohee, when I am alone,
I may string the phial and hang it with my talisman—
a red fox paw—around my neck. With my every step
the crystal could beat beside the paw there near my heart.
I might absorb the red and orange, orange, orange,
oil of orange. I could become the warmest woman
of my clan. I would have to remember to contain
the heat of such arrogance with a cool, certain
and delicate balance of modesty.

Thinking such thoughts, I wrapped the phial
in my softest fur piece, and slid it inside one glove
to keep it safe as I pulled the other on. The heat of orange
essence pulsed through the fur into my open palm—
and seemed to flow through my skin, into my veins—
until I felt myself become a phial, and prayed
someone would find me sore to lose.

Kayla's Thoughts During a Stormy Ritual Separation

These waters now falling down
with so much fury and violence
do not fill me with such harsh emotion.
My body is full of water and blood.

I have listened with care to the wind-sound
and the rain-strike. I do not complain
to be sent away in the dearth of the moon,
to seclude myself because the others have fear.

The earth absorbs my flow even when the sky
opens up like a great eye that cries after howling,
and my blood has already gone to feed old roots
that have been long limp and reaching.

I am not afraid to embrace my own body.
I am not fearful of the red-green ground.
I part my lips and still thirst
regularly.

Scraping moon signs into the wall
takes longer when the moon is round
and wood is wet. It will take longer
with these waters now falling down.

How the Conjure Woman Took Her Last Lover

The image came to her in a dream.
She knew his name and the name
of the woman beside him. She watched
her dream self write the two names
in charcoal beside the bed where
the sleeping couple embraced.

When the conjure woman woke up,
she wrote down the names
on an old scrap of paper.
She swept up some dirt
from the bare floor of her hovel
near her bed, and rolled the paper
around it. Then she set it all on fire
to burn the love of the couple away.

She mumbled the man's name
and one of her own secret names
over and over, until the dirt glowed
and mingled with the ashes.
When these had cooled, she wrapped
them in red fabric, twined braided strands
of her first lover's hair around the ashen package,
tied it up and let it hang from her neck
touching her chest beneath her garments.
All day it moved with her rhythms
and remained warm.

That night, she made her blood flow
from her wrist and mixed the ashes
into the small rivulet spilling into her left palm.
She stirred with a straw until the mixture was thick
enough to write the man's name on her skin—
in the palm of her right hand she would
soon slip under her head—thick enough to make

loving red/black letters circle the nipple
of her left breast—to let the letters dip
into her navel and flow on down . . .

The letters of her most secret name she puzzled
in matrimony with this new man's name
on her inner thighs. She caused these names to seep
around her legs and ankles, adding
more blood to help the letters run together.
Then, she carefully stopped
her blood's flow and wiped clean
the bottoms of her feet. She wanted
nothing on her soles so she would be free
to dance the wildest dream dance:
> the dance that would make more
> than the man's feet tingle; the dance
> that would make his woman turn cold;
> the dance that would conjure him
> to her bed, where he would find her
> blazing for him.

Many things could melt
in the fires of her dreams, but he would
never burn with his now consecrated name.
When he appeared she would take
him in completely. She called out
the dream man's new name before
she permitted herself to sleep.
He would come. She was certain.
Tonight she would be able to put the parts
together as he had never known before—
firm, and real, and fully whole—
wholly of her being.

J.T. Gets the Small-Town, Star-Struck, Wonder Why Blues

When Corina wears red she sings the blues
down at SloAnne's Club. She walks on stage
with smoky eyes aglow and the band is cued.
She sings:
                "I want to tell you
                How I feel
                Words escape me
                From time to time. . ."

Tonight, she is solid—red head to toe—
and the flash of flesh is a pearl delight.
Her blues come on to me. My body cries.
She sings:
                "Your eyes invite me
                To open up to you
                I open my arms
                Waiting for your move

                Wonder why
                I can't tell
                I've got the blues

                Do you want 'em, Baby
                Wonder Why
                I can't tell
                I've got the blues"

My loud admiration drowns as she steps
into the whistling din, skirts reaching hands
and walks towards me. My hands work fast to grab

her a chair. We sit. A new act comes on—
triplets, and no one pays us any mind.
"I've seen those checkered skirts," I say, "but you

are from someplace. Where?" Pure Sugar, she laughs,
"New Orleans, Chicago . . . You name a place,
but here I am." "You sure are," I say, thinking

fast, still wondering how to get a taste
of her blues on my tongue. She sees my smile.
"The song is all you get," she says, and leaves.

Mountain Storm In Flat Shoals

His motorcycle hidden in the bushes,
we ease down the muddy bank,
and hear rumbling cars roll fast above our heads.
Beneath the bridge of the busiest back road
around this scenic mountain town,
Little River flows along my thighs,
and J.T. is lightning—flashing brilliant,
his pale, bare skin reflecting water
blinding-silver—in my eyes. I look away.

The sun drops her slanting gold on me and him.
I watch our shadows move as we make
cold waves splash up and crash on slick gray rocks
and brown-green moss. This is a spring surge
before the stillness summer heat will bring,
a primitive drive, a chance to take when winter-slick asphalt
no longer gleams with frost and forming ice.

This is the result of a pent-up longing, and hope,
this strange need to experience everything out in the open,
while the world is great and green and the mountains
still rise up with their rock hard insides rolling against
the machines, roiling against the flatness, diamond dust
blinding-silver—in my eyes. I look away.

Later, we head out away from the new plateaus and keep riding
until the dark hides that new horizon lately forced upon us—
our mountain tops in the hollers, the rivers missing their beds.
The cry is high and lonesome. Where is the soothing balm?
Primitive measures mean a temporary fix, like poking
steel wool in a rat's hole to prevent access. What can be done
about the rats who are stealing the star stuff from our souls?

Cinderella's Prince In Salem, South Carolina

I was sitting ever so lightly
at the top of the porch steps
in my shortest red skirt,
and checked halter top—
my high heels clicking
with a rhythm I couldn't get
out of my mind.

The August day was dog hot
and just heating up,
when he provided a brilliant shade.
My thoughts were racing
after his magic: *"Hello."*

I tagged a lazy "Hey" behind his greeting,
not bothering to stand or offer him a seat.
Then I smiled and leaned back—you know,
the way I'd learned looked so fetching,
and inquired of him: "J.T.?"

He drew out the "m"s in his *"Ummm Hmmm?"*
until I could almost feel them vibrating on my skin.
    "Suppose you rode up
    on your magnificent motorcycle,
    and I was alone, in a bath . . .
    with a bottle of gin . . ."

He was warming up to the
tall tale, his body leaning down,
reaching for mine.

"Why not Jim Beam?" he asked,
but I'd had this planned to be gin.

I reached up, putting my finger on his lips
and he hushed as I continued: "my glass
          slippery . . ."

I raised one foot high in the air.
His right hand captured and held
my leg but his left hand wouldn't stay put.
So, I pulled back, and he sat down
beside me where the stoop was nice and narrow.
His hardness pressed my back against the rails.

    "*Get along, Cindy.*" He urged.

    "My glass slippery . . . and" I added, "full."

    "*Then what?*" He moaned.

   "No." I said,
and then I gave him an invitation
he didn't really need:
   "Now, you tell me,
      and we'll put the parts together."

J.T. said: "*I say, swallow it all
          and let the gin sing.*"

And I thought I would smile
until the sun went down.

Red Shoes In the Appalachian Mountains

It didn't matter that Mama's hands were tired
from working at her sewing machine all day,
from peeling potatoes into a pot on the wood stove
for supper, from her countless daily chores.
Friday night she would tie on our shoes
and clap her hands for us to dance.
She would sing songs handed down, or make up things
to help us find new clogging rhythms.
      "God bless us all," Mama said, "if dancing is the sin
      Our new, young preacher makes it out to be."
At night I prayed for shoes that wouldn't hurt my toes,
red ones, as shiny as my old black ones had been.
I dreamed of pearly gates a swinging open,
a music playing with a rhythm I could understand,
me and my whole family all white-robed dancing in,
my feet a bright red blur beneath a brand new hem.

Unnatural Cage

My wild, monkey-eyed mother,
I remember the crazed look
in your blameless brown eyes
when Brother passed the flashlight
over them in the dark fields.

You running away,
taking me and Little Sister hostage
against your confirmed escape.
Brother thought us animals—
with his dim light he confused
our eyes with the wild eyes of dogs.
What the neighbors thought with us
on their doorstep later I can not guess.
When Daddy found us, I was still
trying to hide my wet dress-tail,
my brand-new oxfords and lace socks,
all urine soaked. I had to pee, Mama,
and you told me not to move.

There are no iron bars
around the damned past
I try to reach you through.
Tell me why you were running
in your stockings, brown work shoes,
and that striped-taupe dress you made.
Tell me why your eyes
look like old glass eyes
on a doll I once upon a time
left out in the rain.

Sound Sense

His hoe scraped hard dirt
as I finished the sentence
and turned a page. I thought
Daddy wanted me to feel guilty
for not helping him with the work.
So, I blamed myself, pushing my way
through endless rows, continuing to read.

He leaned the hoe against
my open window, with a thud
that made the window rattle.
I looked up and out at the garden,
as if I expected him to be there
standing like the corn forever,
tall and green.

He kicked against the porch steps
loosening the dirt that would be there
and on the floor inside for Mama
to sweep up before dark—a superstition.
I had to read—ignore the distractions.
Fall was fast approaching
I had so much to learn.

He came toward my room,
and stopped at the door.
Words couldn't matter.
I knew he was leaning there
in the hall, like the hoe outside my window.
He knew I'd been reading but he stood there,
always expecting more.

The Ritual Changes

Aunt Mona used to sing her mind while we picked fruits and vegetables. When words wouldn't come she would hum. The sound seemed to help us fill our hands, our bowls, our jars, our bodies. The sound was part of my life. I craved a soft ballad about a young girl, growing up, and Mona singing in her faded calico blueberry dress—stained from making preserves. I asked her to sing that song to me again, while we crocheted on the porch years later with blue yarn just the right color for my memory. She had forgotten. I snatched at the tune, the words haunting me from long green days far gone. I sang them when they came—not fresh and round and crowned, like Mona's berry voice—but like an empty dress, hanging dry, flapping in the wind:

> Walk down to the water and look in.
> It looks so deep. Walk down to the water
> and wave to yourself. Then dip your dear
> hand in and taste the deep water
> flowing down from the mountains
>   where you have roamed.
> You'll taste the coolness of ages
>   of labor, as water seeps
> through dirt and roots where they've grown.

I drank some lemonade while Mona quietly laughed. She gathered up more yarn, saying, "I made up things like that when I was young. Sure, and I loved that dress, though, it was 'most see-through the summer I met Clarence." We continued crocheting in silence, broken only by bird song, buzzing insects, squeaky chains—and Uncle Clarence coughing s'much that we could hear him all the way to the porch from the back bedroom where he was laid-up with another injury from the rock quarry. I tried to crochet some of the song into my mind so I could write it down, maybe put it in a poem later—not to forget, chain one, not to forget, half-double—slip stitch, not to forget.

Squeak, squeak. Return to Mona saying the swing needed a new chain. Everything needed to be fixed around here. The blue paint was peeling off the porch ceiling. I kept thinking about the wind and wanting to hear Mona sing back yesterday, until she asked me if I was planning on getting married anytime soon, and she grew as old as I had just been young. I didn't want to think of being tied down, or stuck in a rut. I didn't know what I was going to do. Looking from up my yarn to the rusty links holding us up, I cleared my sticky throat, and—dying for water—saw Mona's blue dress disappear. I thought I could make do alone just fine, I told her. I said that I didn't need a man who might hold me back. Everybody could stand a little holding, she said. Then Mona remembered that Clarence needed his breathing treatment. The fog rose and I felt the cool air grow thick. Beads of water formed on all the chains and settled on top of everything, like morning dew. I wiped my face, blessed myself, put away my yarn and thought about coursing away from the hills like so much water.

What I Was Told About the Fire On the Mountain

Francie went flouncing her checkered skirts and thin petticoats
from the kitchen into the living room where shine-drunk men
played cards and laughed. She asked: "Do y'all want anything?"
She didn't mind their narrow eyes, their drooling lips;
she didn't mind their outstretched hands, their fingers
reaching—but I sure enough know her mama did.

I was told that Francie's mama went in to stop the ruckus,
and to put Francie back to work in the kitchen, cutting biscuits.
Her mama must have mumbled under her breath, the way
the stories say she was want to do: "I wish your sister would
come on along with my stove wood. You girls know
how to dawdle more 'n all else."
"Now, Mama," Francie would have laughed,
saying: "You know that's not all true."

Mara had been outside all day working with the men,
her arms like metal cords; Francie had been cooped up
inside cleaning floors, washing clothes and dishes—
cleaning herself up before the men came home.
Hearing Francie laugh, they might have complained
that the room was getting too cold. "I'll just go stoke the fire,
and be right back," She may have told her mama,
who had her hands in a bowl of new bread dough.

She wasn't a bright girl, Francie.
She may have thought of saving time
to flirt; she reached and got the kerosene,
lifted the heater lid, and poured the liquid in.
The blazes shot up and caught her hair on fire.
They say she screamed dropping the whole can
in the heater, splashing her bodice and skirts, and all
caught fire just as her mama ran into the room.

Francie was her baby. What could she do?
The drunkards laughed, watching the clothes burn
off Francie's body. Crying out for help, "Lord!"
Francie's mama wrapped her floured arms around her daughter.
When Mara rushed into the flaming house, it was too late
to save her mama or Francie. Both had inhaled the flames
and could no longer breathe; Francie was charred, and some say
she was also showing bone. The men still held their jugs and cards.
Mara threw her load of wood at the gaping men
and made them scatter, wrapping the dying women
together in a blanket from the couch.

The story goes that Mara put out the fire and saved the house.
Some tellers hint at murder or suicide. Dumb luck is more likely.
Still, the sheriff must have had a lot of work to do that night.
They say sometimes he has to visit Mara's place up on the hill,
but most folks know to leave her alone because she can sure go crazy.
Kin or no kin, drunk or sober, they'll stay out in the yard, if they come
by at all.

Crazy Threads Speak

When I could no longer be a sheet, I became a dress for Maura.
Her mother, Lonnie, sewed the tear and dyed me a delicious red.
I was cut from a pattern made by Maura's grandmother.
Lonnie thought about her own favorite dress and sewed rickrack
and lace around the hem and sleeves. She finished me off with
buttons for the back, and four in a row for decoration on the bodice.
Maura loved me, so I wanted to grow with her.
Too soon I trailed above her knees.

When I could no longer be the required length for Maura,
I became a hand-me-down for Louise. Louise hated me from the
start. She didn't want her older sister's dress.
Lonnie tried to make me more appealing. She appliquéd roses on
the bodice, replacing the buttons. Louise picked at the rickrack
and lace, until Lonnie edged the hems in floral cotton of varied
shades of red. I was never happy with Louise.
She showed me envy in possession.

When I could no longer be made to suit Louise,
I became material, waiting in a trunk, to be put to some good use.
The trunk was full of different kinds of cloth, holding smells
soap-water wouldn't wash away. We were never closed up long,
but I remained in waiting some time after Lonnie died.
I was glad to have heard Maura's father asking Lonnie
who should have the sewing things, and quilts.
Her weak response was "Maura. Louise buys her bedding."

When I could no longer be contained, I became a found thing
as I leaped into Maura's hands. "My old dress!"
was the first thing she exclaimed. "Remade for Louise.
Well. La-de-da!" She held me to her chest and twirled around.
I knew her heartbeat was my own right then.
"Let's see what I can do with you."
She proudly spread me back out on the bed.
I hadn't been a sheet for so long I had almost forgotten

the softness of a bed, but Maura looked at me
thinking of comfort, knowing what I would best become.

Maura took everything from the trunk, and repaired the quilt
Lonnie had used on her marriage bed, replacing what was in tatters.
I was made into a center red-rose appliqué, and Maura put her
mother's roses in the corners. I had never looked more beautiful.
Maura used me carefully on her bed. I was spread out in the
morning, and nightly folded down to the foot—for use only on the
coldest nights. When I needed to be laundered, Maura did this, too,
with care. She hand washed me—no squeezing—and hung me with
many pins, dripping, in the shade of trees to dry, so the sun would
not fade my colors. Once, when I was almost dry, Louise brought her
children for a visit. I became gatekeeper for the day. Maura gently
spread me, top-under, over the latch, then they left the children
outside to play.

As the visit ended, I could no longer bear to go unnoticed.
I became the object of Louise's attention. I made myself difficult
to manage when Maura lifted me, trying to fold me wrong-side out
so the roses wouldn't show. A fold fell open, and Louise was a hawk.
"Hey! Is that a rose from my old dress?" Maura shuffled children
through the gate. "No. It's from my old dress. Remember?" I
became a relic for the closet after that—taken out, admired and
loved, but seldom used.

Hidden in the closet, I learned about fear. Maura suspected
I would be taken, so she covered me with crocheted blankets
and lace doilies. As time drew on, I worried when the door opened
and white hands reached into the dark corner where I was folded.
I didn't know if the hands would belong to Maura, and I had learned
what ownership could mean. I cowered when I didn't burn with
rage: strange, ungainly powers, ghostly dormant. Maura has every
right to be afraid. Crazy quilts are too popular to be tucked away.
Why, I've even heard that some people frame them and hang them
like fine art these days.

Telling Time

An infernal buzzing made Ona-Mae remember
she hated flies—not for being household pests.
She hated flies because of maggots.
Ona had once loved the feel of tiny feet
as ants crawled in her hands, and up her arms.
She laughed when Cousin Molly brushed them off,
pulling her back to the shelter of the trees—
away from the sand and gravel in the road.
She cried into the clover before looking near the stems
for the little people Molly told her about.

Molly said clover hid little fairy-like dream-takers
like kudzu hid snakes. The little people liked to watch
our large faces twitch at the movement of their hands.
Dream-takers could touch our eyelids and know
our dreams. Ona-Mae often pretended to sleep—
to catch the dream-people in the act, but sleep
was a swift creeper in her eyelashes weaving them closed.
She slept and woke with buzzing in her ears.

Molly said bees would not sting people
who did them no harm. She said bees were full
of useful information. Some day Ona would understand.
One nice big bee held good news of strawberry season;
another buzzed by saying it was time to go inside.
Flies came in through holes in screens, or gathered
near doors to be let in. Puzzled, Ona watched
grown-ups swat and fuss. "What had the flies said?
What had they done?" she wondered. When fall came
Ona went to school. She was glad to outgrow
the need for Molly and her soft, sleepy voice
that always made Ona feel like dreaming.
Cousin Molly never got in trouble for telling
stories that grown-ups often called lies.

One night that winter, Ona's family watched
a television program about poor foreign people
needing food. Ona saw children with big bellies
reaching for brown bowls full of white stuff,
and she thought the rice she had never seen
was worms. Mama said, "No, Ona. Those kids
are hungry, but they wouldn't eat worms."
Yet, Ona saw them eating flies.
The flies were swarming in the rice bowls.
The children licked flies that were crawling
on their lips, into their mouths. The children scooped
into their humming bowls with hungry fingers.
That night, Ona dreamed of worms and flies.

She didn't think about the children after Christmas.
She forgot the flies until they started coming in again.
The flies would wake her up late mornings buzzing
by her ears. She, too, began to shoo them all away.
Once, Ona woke thinking about the dream-takers
of preschool days, and her Cousin Molly. She found a fly
had been crawling on her arm. Sleepy, Ona was reminded
of even softer ant feet and she let the fly crawl, drifting back
into sleep, covering her ears against the buzz.

That summer, Ona found old Mama Cat covered
in cooked white rice. Shading her eyes, she could see
Mama Cat moving underneath the mound.
Ona ran to uncover Mama Cat, confused by the hungry
worms, the bloody fur and bones she saw—
and Mama Cat not really moving.
Her father came out to her when he heard her scream.
He cleaned her up, and held her while she cried.
He said it was time.

Moma Cat was old. Her time was up.
He said, "I'll get the shovel." Ona gathered stones.

He covered Moma Cat with dirt and bordered the mound.
Ona asked her father to say a few words. He said, "It's no use. . ."
Ona's face forecasted tears, "until we're finished here."
Her father made a cross of twigs and grass.
Then he removed his hat and said, "This here cat lived
long enough to have more kittens and kill more
things than any other cat I've ever owned.
I hope she didn't suffer long, and I wish I'd gotten
to her before the maggots." He shoved his hat back on.

He had made Ona-Mae feel proud. She hoped someone
would treat her so well someday. Such kind words....
When Ona asked, her father told her the whole truth
about flies—how they had to come from maggots.
His fingertips were rough on soft skin beneath her eyes,
but Daddy's was a touch she now adored.
That night, she went to sleep and dreamed
of Daddy's hands on her face, and the big watch
on his wrist as it loomed near her eyes.
The next day she took his huge, rough hand in hers,
and asked him if he would teach her to tell time.

Seasoning

Bone white on the kitchen table,
a spill of salt, a superstition:
I toss a pinch
over my shoulder,
where the moon
always is in love poems,
and nothing happens.
I can inhale.

Curiosity bubbles like brew
in some hidden cauldron,
and I unscrew the lid,
the cold, stainless steel top
of the shaker, on purpose
to pour a small, white mountain.
It moves when I breathe.

Thinking of all the experts
who have used
this common crystalline structure
to illustrate the complexities of our universe,
I begin to examine
the grains found in so many things
the way a budding, young scientist might.
I lean in closer, and jar the table.
What a mess I've made.

A trail of salt shapes itself into a wing
as part of the mountain collapses.
I decide to poke my finger in
the part that is still standing,
and feel like a giant
who has done something wrong.

I make a swirling pattern
as a memory rises
and my kitchen seems far away
while I rake my fingers through the salt.

I went into Grandpa's cold salt-room,
and saw a large, dead pig on the table.
The room smelled old and rusty,
but everything the light hit
was shining like new hard candy.
The table was covered
with gritty, beautiful stuff.
Some of the big crystals
had large red, jewel-like flecks.
I wouldn't admit to tasting the salt
back then, but I did and almost died—
I was so sick that night, messing up mama's lap.
Nothing would stay inside and I was shaking—
so white and cold—and Lord have mercy,
I don't know what preserved me.

In my kitchen,
I scrape the swirls into my hands,
and go wash up.
Collecting the last minute grains
with a damp dishcloth,
I notice how shiny and tight
the salt has made my skin.
I brush back my hair
and touch the corner of my eye.
I will have to sweep the floor later.
Rotten luck!
Salt's in my eye right now
and I can't see a thing.

Montage of Days

Rise to wash up hands and faces
Morning comes in bits and pieces
Coffee cups in saucers or glasses of milk
Pats of butter in full plates of hot grits
Buttered warm bread to sop it all up with
Sweet mouthfuls of stuff just to hold us over
Early whirling round with tall grass bending
Whipping brown hair breaking summer's vision
Dizzy in the slanting sun and blooming clover
Up jumps a rabbit in the red hot pokers
Whistling flags and buttercup noses
Noon dandelions and a bunch of wild roses
Long blades of grass and lady slippers
Cold well water sipped from a dipper
None too fast and none too slowly
Split breakfast biscuits left out on the stove
Spoon in sugar, jelly or mayonnaise
Get a little something out from a tin
Safe in a cabinet in the far kitchen
Orange blossom daylilies in jar vases
Open and close with a graceful fragrance
Glaring green June bug on a white string
Counting each loop made while circling
Writing with straws poked in purple berries
Making mud pies and cakes or cookies
Tasting muscadines and honeysuckle
Coming to the table when called for supper
Filling in the corners by taking a dip
A dusting from the lid on the bottom lip
Going back out to the yard in twilight
Taking dares or seeking fireflies
Stepping in persimmons under the tree
Walking in high grass to clean off feet
Sheets all brought fresh off the line

Eventide beds made just in time
For stories or songs to drift off by
Being ever so thankful for such another day
Waking up thinking of such another day

Kudzu and a Question Under Moon Shine

Can you hear me well? Am I speaking plain?
I have been drinking shine in deep kudzu.
I know the dangers. You know I've held snakes—
mostly green and black, though. They won't kill you.
Your church could hold revivals in this field.
I'd tell your friends to keep their copperheads.
We could get some shine that's been through copper,
and bless our souls, and sanctify our dead.

They wouldn't go for that, and it's as well.
By God, some things are better off not mixed.
I feel exotic here with this strange plant,
admired for its beauty and hand-picked
with care. Transported as a ground cover,
it soon grew out of bounds in this hot land.
They tried domestication, cutting back;
kudzu grew less admired and more be damned.

Still, something could be said for the strength
to strangle a tree, to embrace a barn.
I feel the power coil around my foot.
Were it your snake, I would be less alarmed.
It seems this kudzu knows what I have thought,
so I am touched with empathy. Won't you
join me here? Be less afraid than I am.
I've seen you handle fire. Walk through kudzu.

What would you do if I held you in Faith?
Let me anoint your head with my lips. Come,
what works for me is Works in this dark place.
Follow me, and we will find our way home.

Walking—My Way

The sun's long rays shine through the drying leaves.
Walking through the woods, I hear crackling
on the tree limbs and underneath my feet,
though there is no wind, and I step softly,
hating to disturb intricate patterns—
the sunshine on the leaves—and their small veins.

With each step, my blood rushes through my veins.
I can feel it pound through me as it leaves
my heart in that ancient thump-thump pattern.
I am not afraid, but tension crackles
in the air. With breath, I stir it softly
and moving now I crush it with my feet.

I am alone, but I know many feet
have passed along this ridge and the ravine.
None seem to make a harmful mark. Softly,
we walk separate paths, secure in leaving
no trace—or anything to start crackling
fires out of control. I respect patterns

I observe in Nature—hidden patterns
with rhythm, rhyme, reason, and some with feet.
I hear noises as everything crackles
alive with the sun's warmth in well-fed veins.
Almost nothing escapes me. Yet, I leave
something of me here. It happens softly.

Picking up a leaf, I rub it softly,
watching my lean fingers trace the pattern.
I note quietly the beauty of leaves,
and think, again, of my own hands and feet,
attached to limbs—crisscrossed by stem like veins.
Strange, that these appendages don't crackle.

Sometimes age makes bones begin to crackle,
like the leaves, and skin will fall so softly
into folds—bruises come easy and veins
burst open, drawing shaded blue patterns.
Not yet, for me. No matter if my feet
try to make me feel age—make me believe.

Fresh—new and old life in my veins, I leave,
knowing that patterns have shifted softly,
and much crackles beneath my restless feet.

In the Absence Of Light

—written upon hearing of Carl Sagan's death

it makes sense
that there are no colors,
no banded spectrum
to illustrate the elemental
nature of all matter;
it makes sense
that we can know
every thing and no thing
so well by calculation,
and by observation
of such intricate repetition;
it makes sense
that our ancestors were
afraid of the dark, hungry mouth—
night, a gaping black hole taking faith,
a fierce abandonment
of the known;
it makes sense
that we still seek
the billions and billions
of answers to questions
expanding relatively
with the speed
of thoughts. . .

Learning To Take Positions

I sit in tall grass near the trees at the edge
of the field and wait, looking into underbrush—
not at waves the wind makes. Not looking,
I listen for him in the unquiet, feeling heat
waft from the sun-warmed ground. I take etched
stones from my apron pocket, from their pouch,
and place them face down in the recommended circle,
humming a song I once heard the conjure woman sing.

A small tuft of grass works its way into my hands.
I shake root dirt out of my lap onto the stones
turning three over to read the open and closed
triangles, and the single center arrow pointing up.
Have I done the right thing, by going to conjure woman?
I have tried to get J.T.'s attention all summer.
He pays the cows more mind than he pays me.
Wiping my palms, I gather my stones, and brush off the dirt.
Putting my pouch back in my pocket, I close my eyes
and whisper, "I don't care if he comes or not."

Did I lose my senses? The whole field grew quiet.
My breathing became constricted, dry, tight.
He didn't walk softly. He didn't tremble
to make a visible path through my father's field
turning to honey-brown hay. I could hear dry grass break
and still green grass bend. I could hear the alarm
of insects holding on until blade met blade.
The swishing, whirring sound when winged-life leapt away.
I felt the pelting of so many tiny feet before his hand
came into view. When did I open my eyes?

He touched my cheek. I looked into his widening
gaze and smiled reassuringly at him. He plucked
a large grasshopper from my hair. Our bodies
throbbed with more than life's blood, more than fear.

I watched the green insect he let go regain her legs
and bound away. The stalk of grass returned to wait
again. My fear had been released—he took it up,
searching the trees for something—someone who might
see. I undid my bodice to regain his wild eyes.
The undergrowth held mystery. I held far more.

Haven

    Written after reading Robert Penn Warren's "Law of Attrition"

I have learned the law
of attrition, Dear Sir.
I have felt fists—gavels—
strike blows. This is not
natural—not nature's mountain,
or her grain of sand,
This law is the law of man.

If you will just
hear me out. I say
let the men beat
drums. Let them wage
strange wars against
the decline of man.
Let Robert Bly forge Iron,
and let us women rise up
and join with the men.
Women can beat drums—
they held drums before
bowls and baskets were
positioned to be filled.

In terms of safety, yes,
I am all for some kind
of asylum, you mention
one where no foot may
peacefully come.
Let us walk
there together and stand
near the edge, exploring
the sharp, smooth facets—

the mountain in the sand—
with drums and hands
held silent, one day, suddenly,
agreeably realizing unity.

  "We make the path by walking."
    —Robert Bly, *Iron John*

The First Star Out

Sometimes, I think my only existence is his.
When he says he hears a whisper of stars,
I see them—I hear them in his voice.

And when I think of him in the distance, far
from the reach of my call, I feel fear,
knowing we are one body—a mass of flesh, our

arms reaching for stars. We begin to hear
them speak in different tones, with different meanings.
How can they start to pull us apart when it took years

for us to become so nearly together? I try to dismiss
these thoughts when night comes. In the starlight I feel free
enough with the first star out to make a gleaming wish.

When the other stars appear in brilliance through night clouds,
I'd have to try to hear them whisper. How lovely that they're loud.

Whisper Will

With her bed so near the window
she can hear crickets hit the screen
and click into position
wings and knees,
moist music, filtered
rhythms in cool air.

She pulls the thin sheet to her waist,
watching water drops gleam
into one square after another,
reaching the sill. Sleep falls
into waking like the water drops,
like night into day. Soon the sun will be
over the ridge; a night hawk dips
above the damp ravine.

Haunting sound, a Whip-poor-will,
so far away he seems
to be whispering,
and her heart beat is too loud
with her hand beneath her pillow.
        "Quiet, please.
         Quiet, please."
She can hear the dainty twang
as crickets leave the screen.

Night Echoes, and Morning

I think of my first lover,
the death of my father
and sex with any man,
in just that order.
"Please," I say,
wanting to stop.

I think of sex
with my new lover,
pain, and how healing
love can be.
"Please," I say,
wanting more.

I think of discussions
about death, stupid advice,
and having to rise
each morning.
"Please," I say,
wanting to rest.

I think of my body,
"The Temple of the Lord"
longing for worship, communion,
lying naked between the sheets.
"Please," I say,
wanting some response.

Twilight:
night stretches,
reaching into the light, like fingers
clawing for the small warmth
still on the other side of the bed,
on the other side of sleep.

Breathing While He Sleeps

At the window Maurine wonders
why anyone is sleeping, wishing she could
go outside to walk among the shadows—below. . . .
Across the street, her neighbor has left
his shade open. Her eyes are drawn.

His curtains hang sprinkled with dew. His room must
smell of stale cigar smoke, stubs in the tray, and sweat—
lots of it—the muscled "macho" man is huge. He takes
his cowboy hat off and tonight he is completely naked.

Watching the yellow curtain make damp waves
back and forth as his hand bumps into it, Maurine
rests a hand on her chest. She almost wants to wake
her husband to have him look, to let him in. . .
Maurine stumbles, catching her breath, feeling dizzy.

For, suddenly she has realized that her neighbor was the man
she couldn't identify a long while back when he was draped
in the yellowed newspaper down at the laundromat.
Her friends all said strangers probably made fast lovers
in movies that he craved and she was a stranger
he had wanted for a long time. Her friends had said
he must have watched her to learn her moves—
how and where she would carry herself.
No one would have ever guessed that they had been
as close as neighbors, nodding at each other
when they couldn't nod at night—never this naked,
just a hint of flesh, a breath of night air to make
a person love what fills the lungs.

Her neighbor began quietly the day he showed himself
stranger than any other stranger at the laundromat.
Maurine had turned with an unvoiced "Excuse me?"
on her tongue. She felt heat from his naked body rise
on wafted air, and her face begin to flush.

Yes, the hair on her nape lifted. She even screamed,
later wondering why. He had looked so painfully
out of place standing there in his sneaky-boy smile,
the torn newspaper wrapped around his lower body
quickly spreading open for Maurine to view his skin.

When the policeman, wanting a description,
asked for details, Maurine remembered the headline
flashing up first. The bold words "Naked Guns,
Supported by ROC," the fine print blurring
near his hair and skin. "Colors. Ma'am,
do you remember colors?" "Black and White."
Maurine mumbled, her mind drifting
to piles of clothes, and newly-wed hopes
of owning a house, with her own washer and dryer.

The night she and her husband had first moved
into the apartment Maurine stood at the window,
and her husband woke, inviting her back to bed,
loving the light touch of her fingers on his rough skin.
Over time, her touch had changed, became a thin veil.
Maurine told her husband that the wind couldn't know why
it touched the trees in certain ways—at certain times.
She watched their white curtains begin to flutter.

Tonight, she turned away from the window in anger
at not having known her part in this neighborly game—
her neighbor is only wearing that same laundromat smile
she should have known was too familiar. Maurine shivers
in the light falling through her sheer night gown
onto the clean bed covers. There, the mound
that is her husband stretches himself out,
covering his bald head with a pillow—
mate to the one she must hold.
Maurine reaches out for her husband
touching only the warm air around him—
at certain times she can hardly breathe.

Daddy's Now Vacation

Elaine tosses her hair around
and holds it, twisted, on one side
of her long neck. She wants to go
ski—where the mountain, snow packed
this year with the real stuff, waits.
Stuck here in the reptile house
in Hot Springs, Arkansas, she begins
to see herself as a swag lamp—hanging
from a ceiling, turned on and hot . . .
she dangles her legs toward the water.

As she watches the cold blooded
reptiles and the man who brought her here,
Elaine feels her skin slither
in anger on her bones, and she hears
the distant voice of her mother,
reminding her before they left Iowa:
        "You went skiing last year.
        Daddy says the hot new spot
        is down in Arkansas. Make him
        happy, baby. It's such a little thing."

She wants to swing down from the ceiling,
and be free to sizzle on snow not brought
in by trucks, but by God   "Click"
the natural way.   Mama takes a picture.
Here Elaine is handing Daddy a cup
of pure spring water. Daddy laughs,
and reads the cup:
        "Arkansas: The Natural State."
She rolls her eyes while he's not looking,
wondering what could be natural about being
in this Godforsaken place.
        "I thought this was supposed to be 'The Land
        of Opportunity,' didn't you?" Daddy asks.

She has her chance, but looks at Mama
and decides not to knock Daddy's idea of fun.
Instead, she says, baby-sweet,
   "That's what we were supposed to learn in school."
Elaine thinks hard, searching for an opportunity to escape.

Falling Over Reptiles

When Elaine cooled off, she actually began
to enjoy the forced vacation and the visit
to the reptile house. After all, she couldn't ski
in a leather skirt, and it was fun to sit on the precipice
showing her thighs, knowing just what the sandy-
haired, tan man who had been following them
eagerly leaned forward to see.

Distracted by his new cam-corder and her mother's prattle,
Elaine's father didn't see her when she slid too close
to the rocky edge of the alligator pit and almost fell.
The tan man rushed forward, reached out
and pulled her backwards so hard that she landed
on his snake skin boots. His fingers left imprints
on her arms. His rich, wild scent
coiled around her.

Her father's "Now, now, Young Lady" lecture was like ice
melting into spring water. She let it dissolve as the man
lifted her up, bracing her close until she made herself
pull away. The pain from the bruise forming on her leg
was nothing compared to the burn in her chest
from the look in the tan man's eyes. Sure.
He was concerned. So were her parents.

Elaine, reading him, didn't respond
to their traditional questions:
    "Are you O.K.? What were you thinking?"
He would think of her as just another dumb blonde
he could grab. He would see her as easy,
when all she wanted was a little thrill—
a bright ski sweater, the reflective, gold fringe
of the lodge swag lamps, the firm, tightness
of just the right snow. He would remember her
as the girl he'd seen falling over reptiles,
if he remembered her at all.

Priority Mail

Dear, Mother,
I send this quick note to say
that my weekly lengthy letter
in response to yours
will be late this time
because I mailed it early.

This morning I read
about the mail truck
lying in a river bed.
The driver fell asleep
and lost control.
Although the old saying
says nothing
about river bed crashes,
I am sure your letter will be fine.

The reporter said
they couldn't break
the seal on the heavy truck
before they pulled it out.
No U. S. Official was on hand
to authorize the matter.
Seven wreckers were called in—
Mother—what a lucky number,
and they had to have a path
cleared to get to the truck,
which had navigated through
the trees without disturbing
any limbs or trunks. No wide-
awake driver wanted to attempt
such an astounding feat.

It took all day and still more waiting.
When the U. S. Official arrived
and found no mail damaged,
he sent it on its merry way.
You should get your letter soon.
At least it's not drifting
downstream, and I promise
this time all these hurried
words are true. With love,
always, Your Daughter.

The Perfect Candidate

All week she worked in the warehouse deep freeze,
dressed in the warmest clothing she could find.
She was trying to mold and shape from ice
the perfect horse to photograph
for a two-page spread in *Wild Horse* magazine.

Each of her efforts had sadly collapsed
and lay piled in fragments and bits in corners.
The heads and legs were the most solid.
Nostrils flared, icy eyes fumed and the legs
of frozen water seemed stirred to leap and run.

As she released the last catch on the mold,
she held her smoky breath and stood stock still.
No cracking. Good. This one might make it.
She adjusted the lighting and began to shoot.

The freezer was large, but still
she had to stretch and maneuver
to get the full horse and none of the failed attempts.
She had taken several photos when the horse
on the platform fractured and caved in.

Before she left she straightened up the freezer.
She carted out the platform and the special mold,
then she raked out the scattered fragments
of her week's creation to let them melt
and drain away outside the door.

Taking off her parka she remembered
she had some extra film and took a shot
of the seven horse heads
and twenty some odd surviving legs
jutting out above the rubble of their bodies.

She stayed to take more pictures of the melting,
and the melting sequence made it into the magazine.
In the bottom right hand corner was a photo
of water running into an ice cold drain.

Irregular Trinity

They are so beautiful, the poison vines
that weave through shrubs to creep along stone walls.
I want to trace their patterns with my hand,
to reach for stems that twine a siren song.

Alarm breaks out in me to leave them be
as sunlight glares now from their shining green.
I voice, "Don't blind me with such glancing light,
for I did not uproot you in your youth
and I won't blight you in your adult prime."

Is this a product of having free will—
stretching toward the light for life and support
only when a certain darkness is known?

In my small garden, I ponder with faith—
all chaos and creation—pro and con,
for I have been afraid to fall asleep—
afraid I would not wake to see the sun.

I am full of longing for more kindness.
Who knows what may not live and what may thrive?
They are so beautiful, these poison vines
stirring up my blood, my body and my mind.

When She Had Too Much To Drink At the Fall Party

She thought about her teacher's tomatoes
and how he had carried the seeds from Rome,
he said, all the way home in his front pocket,
where the packet was sure to be too warm.

Party guests were served fried green tomatoes,
the last of the season. He saved some seeds,
he said, for next spring. She proposed a toast:
To tomatoes—to all that red and green

fruit of the vine, work of his hands, from Rome,
in Arkansas. God, bless 'em. Every one. . . .
She grew as sentimental as her poems.
When she began to slur, he helped her home.

He spoke of how he'd staked tomatoes out
in Arkansas—how he had watched them grow
as he tended them and worked on his tan.
His voice held seasoned hints of anguish, though,

when he described how soon fair skin could burn.
She couldn't speak, although it was her turn,

while plump, perfectly round, red tomatoes
mingled, like guests, with his more lofty thoughts
of sounds in trees, silence and caesuras,
his wife, and those large, erect garden rocks.

Unmeasured Time

Here you are, my daughter,
latched on to my breast,
and this slow release is sensual and good.
I feel the wavy roof of your mouth,
the gentle firmness of your teeth,
the tug and kneading of your soft, rough tongue,
the suction and the pull for sustenance. As you grow
away from me, because of me, so I grow with you.
I create a daughter—you, a mother.

I watch you, wrapped in your skin-warm blanket,
and I know this is a love some people miss.
You slightly smile absorbing the details of my face—
your bright blue eyes probing so much
I have to close my lids. I anoint your silken head
with my lips as your fingers touch my cheek.

Tugging at my ears, my nose, and my lips
can't cause offense. I am only occupied with you.
The telephone's ringer is off, there's no work
makeup to smear, and no party earrings for you
to slip in your mouth. Touch me.
Let me enjoy what will end too soon.
This is our conversation, our interview.
"No interruptions, please."

Your hand at my mouth prevents a flood of words.
I taste your little fingertips and cannot stop
the thought as wild and red as blood:
"I love you so much that I could eat you up."
No one could ever love you any more.
My heart beats faster, our eyes meet.
Are you not afraid?

You give a quickening smile
that positively lingers, calming me down.
I was not as close to you when you were deep inside.
You are here, and I am glad.

Suddenly, I want to see all of you,
knowing I can never take you fully in.
I unwrap your blanket, seeing you have grown.
I am as full of wonder now as you.
Your little body, how can it contain you?
The way our minds inside our heads can hold a house?
You begin to eat again, unhurriedly.
Your eyes close.

You are on your way to sleep.
Again, I'm glad. We both need rest.
The work we do is hard. I think of weaning.
Then, ending conversations with long-
winded people. It takes a lot of effort—
then, you stop, breathe, and swallow.
In a while you will let go or I will
pull away as gently as a mother can.

Reproductions

Mirror, hold my gaze.
Mother me—my face,
my body, my being naked.
My neck leans forward,

shoulders droop from years
of practice hiding height
and small, pointing breasts.
Once, I saw the roundness

of my mother's body, how
she was made from giving
birth, nursing, stooping
in all those fields. I looked
away, and return now
to the image I can bear.

A hand reaches up.
My daughter, still wet
from her bath. I hold
her, loving her skin.

Wrapped in towels, we
brush our teeth, our hair.
We smile and primp, fixing
up each other. I desire no

shame, no jealousy here.
When she says, "Mama,
I wish you had blue eyes
like Daddy and me," my brown
eyes go white. I see
a tiny crack begin to form.

A Funny, Funny Riddle

> "I'll have to keep trying to do it, to die and fly, by words."
> James Dickey—*Self-Interviews*

My Daughter asks:
"How far away is Heaven, Mommy?"

She knows we can't fly there
for a visit. Her Papa flies through
clouds in his small plane,
and now I bet she'll ask him
why some engines quit.

"I don't know, for sure.
I've never been."

"We could get
some magic, and go
through the clouds,
and come back."

She is only four.

I hear her whisper:
"Mama, will you go to Heaven?"
There's a sudden feeling
in my stomach that makes
me think of when she was
inside, a rolling movement.

I say,
"After a very long time, I hope, I may."

I lift her up as she gleams
with a new idea:
"If you do go, jump off

       the clouds before
       you get too high,
       and come back in our door.
       Then, I'll lock it tight;
       that's what I'll do."

"Will, you now?" I ask, giving her a hug.

When she went to sleep,
I wondered what we had
settled. She had been happy
enough to forget the news
that left her mother in tears
as she had passed through
the living room that evening.

Days from now will she remember?
What will she think about
looking at clouds out the car window
while we try to sing John Denver songs
going to visit our mountain folks?

Midnight, and her lashes still
caress her pillowed cheeks.
Almost Heaven....

I find my paper and a pencil; my mind
is on a motorcycle, speeding down
a road I will not name, as I try
to die and fly, by words.
Lord, God, let at least
my fingers find wings.

Some Lines on Snow and Rising Moons

When I lay down in snow beside our child
to make snow angels and saw you smile,
my heart sped back across the miles and years
to the snow-covered yard, the dark white house
of a shut-in neighbor, Mama's old friend.

The night before we'd made love on the floor.
We made the noises we couldn't suppress.
We weren't married, and Mama couldn't allow
this sin to take place again in her house.
It snowed all day. The sky mocked me
with virginal flakes. Later, we went out
on the porch to get some fresh night air.

I heard Mama cough
then pictured her pressed against the door.
"Let's take a walk," I said, so she could hear.
"Don't you two go too far. . . " we heard her say,
as we tracked through the yard.
I was not as cold as afraid. We might wake the neighbor,
give her heart attack, or worse,
she might tell Mama what she saw:
> "He took his coat and placed it on the ground;
> she slipped her pants down just above her knees;
> he kept his at his thighs, and through the steam
> I saw the moon rise several times."

I doubt she would've put it just that way.

When Mama asked about my damp hair,
I said, "I made an angel." Mama sighed.
Inside, I felt like angels were on fire.

Today I want to pull you down with me—
to tell our child to make her own snow man.
But, I rise to see the angels we've made;

to see our beaming daughter look at me;
to feel your arms around my waist, you nudge my hair;
to hear, "I love you;" and to know
just how the moon will rise in our bedroom.

Vacation In the Land Down Under

A white bird in the blue sky
sounds like child's play. I long
to be a new-born baby's mother,
to be so blessed. Almost naked
on this empty stretch of beach,
I see my feet sinking into sand;
becoming more accustomed to
Australia's Family Beaches, I wrap
a mesh sarong around my waist,
and walk toward the familiar music
some family carried in from our native land.
Topless mothers nurse their babies,
topless women walk where children shuffle,
searching for relics they may not get to keep.
Brave fathers try to pay much less attention
to the unfettered women than tourist pamphlets
indicate most men will. The women smile.

There's my daughter, thirteen, too cool
not to be different; too individualistic to try
blending in; her white suit shines
like reflective strips as she leans toward
the water's edge with her camera,
focusing in on what I cannot see.
When I am almost near enough to touch her,
she turns around. So good at sensing me,
she's not at all surprised that I'm no stranger.
After I say, "I'm starved," she says she's not
hungry. I watch her gaze return to the lens
and see her snap up deeply etched symbols
of hope—or witchcraft. Her camera clicks
on tiny rows of prints in the damp sand
where small birds have walked.

As a thin sheet of water ripples over
the image, over our feet, I peer further
down the beach for her father. He is nowhere
to be seen. I look to the blue sky again,
to a white bird sailing so near the sun—I imagine
everyone can hear a paean to Apollo—and I feel
the growling of my empty stomach—my empty womb
I quietly press with both sweaty, gritty palms.

The Residue Of Waves

He holds a seashell to his ear.
Of course, he says he hears the ocean,
sees gulls winding on the air,
and hollowed sand angels
above the creeping tide.
I think of the sun rising on us alone.
We walked in darkness first
to greet the beach before the crowd.
Crabs zig-zagged around before they hid.
Birds walked fully intent before flying.
Prints would suddenly appear and then be gone.

We meandered back to our domed tent.
Not breaking camp as planned, we crawled inside
with clinging salt and sand. Smells of cocoa butter
and night musk had been zipped up with our stuff.
We moved our hiking boots, our staffs, and gear
over to the left and scrambled to unroll a bag.

He had no trouble when he reached for me.
There were no zippers or hooks in his way.
Imagine pearls. Diving. Deep. Inside.
Sky peered through mesh above us and was blue.
I wanted more room. Hot air grew hard to breathe.
I opened the door flap with my toes.

Now, watching him search the shelves for a book,
I want to tell him afternoons are often fine.
First, I put a dab of sunscreen near my ear
and rub my body with lotioned palms.
He still has the seashell in his hand. I touch his back
and let my ocean whisper dance around his neck.
His skin develops Braille as he breathes me in.

Putting the seashell with our box of pictures,
he is so careful that I try not to laugh.
Such tenderness for an object so complex, complete—
that shell just felt the touch of our first date.
His passion lifts me off my feet into his arms.
The bedroom is now a tent I carry in my mind.
We ride the waves that take us to our bed.
Why should I measure height or depth or length?
We ride the waves. We'll contemplate much later.

Beginner Impromptu: Moving With Objects

For dance class, I brought a roll of toilet paper.
She brought a ball and when it rolled out of bounds,
she tossed her wild mane and I lassoed her in a loop
of paper ribbon that she didn't break. She let me

lead her around the others. Then she pulled and pulled
the tissue paper out in streams. I followed her trail,
twisting through trunks and limbs, narrowing down
the scope with the empty cardboard spool.

I spotted her tangled in a multicolored plastic slinky,
and her slanted green eyes suggested that she wanted me
to capture her again. The drums made me feel restless
as I watched her slither in a position that I didn't stop stalking
when the music stopped and the teacher turned us all loose.

Shaking the Tree

She came by the house after dance class
to return a crimson leotard of mine
that had gotten into her bag by mistake.
Her hair was still damp.

I looked at her with her clothes on
and knew the undeniability
of hidden skin. The patio door
was stuck again. Why
had she come around
to the back?

She put her hand up to the latch.
I said, "Wait," too late. We both
got pinched when the latch sprang
and the door inched open.
We soothed our separate
wounds until our eyes met.
The taste of blood still
tender on our tongues.

"Let me see," we said
at the same time, and laughed:
a thin peal, a flash of white and red
and something more delicious—
the thought of what could be yet to come.

My leotard was draped across her wrist.
I stepped outside to take it from her
and when our hands next met we comforted
each other with kisses that did not end
at fingertips and thumbs.

I watched my leotard fall from her arm.
The bed was simply too far away.
Our clothes came off and discovered
potted plants, a stone frog,
a covered grill, an umbrella stand
holding garden tools and a rolled up hose.
The cement was still early-morning-cold.
The glass door slid open,
and we fumbled for soft and warm.

Woman to woman,
was there anything we missed?
When we were as close as two bodies
can get, when we had left nothing else
undone, and were not completely fulfilled—
we didn't really need, or want anything that was not us
to put inside our bodies. We were only too aware
of the physical restrictions—boundaries that minds
like ours could do so well without—
of our soothing, ever soothing, wounded skin.

Sunday Mass—Confusion Of Hands

He complains
about how long it takes me
to get ready for church,
when the alarm is set so early.
He says no one is going
there just to see me.
He's already in his suit
before I fix breakfast.
He thinks we are in a contest.
The clock is ticking,
but he forgets to stack
the dishes in my favor
every time.

"Peace be with you,"
I say to strangers,
after turning from
the peace he offers me.
How many other hands
will he have touched?
I don't count at mass—
I turn a full circle and try
to feel calm before
accepting the bread
as The Body,
and the wine as changed
into: "Blood of Christ."

"Amen," I respond
to the priest, making the sign
of the cross and my way
back to my seat in turmoil.
Sitting beside him I try
to pray calmly, to give thanks,
but the blood in my veins

runs away from my mind
in many nervous circles,
leaving me confused.
And it is almost time
for us to go to "Abba, Father…"
the work of our hands.

Dipped In Autumn

Performance night, open-mic, slam-fest fun . . .
Sauce spreads across the pages and the stage.
To behave or not to behave? What a question . . .
The players make love to their microphones.
Girls dance with whips to tease the enthralled crowds.
Drunken actors blinded by their masks take leave of senses.
They weave about as if they have no bones.
There is no disentangling limb from limb.
Closing time . . . the party ends up at a player's home.
And so it is that many marriages break with day.

And so it is that I am now awake
to stare at scrambled eggs and cold flat cakes.
The coffee swirls. The syrup drips on me.
I ask: "What did I do?" You do not know.
You rise. You eat. You go to work. You sleep.
Do you want to know what goes on in my world?
I want you to know me for who I really am.
I ply in poetry and the stuff of dreams.
I search for truth and beauty—and I lie.
It can be so bleak and ugly here sometimes.

I want to end it all and rise anew.
My stage is back-lit by a falling sun.
Burned, scared, and full of fear I turn to you.
I don't have time to wonder what I've done.
I wonder at you here, my crowd of one.
You must have wanted something off my plate.
It is so cold, but I could warm it up.
Let me just stick it in the microwave.
We'll eat together, then I'll go to sleep,
and wake to dwell on this no more than dream.

Meeting the Crone In the Early Morning

I bow to this wise old woman
because I must,
seeing something familiar in her
knowing reach into the unknown.
It is stored within the marrow.
It is ossified in bone.

I bow to this wise old woman
with winter's face,
her eyes squenched tight
in this half-light, she walks,
an ancient gnarly limb she holds
to rhythmically extend her own.

I bow to this wise old woman
out of respect,
secretly treasuring the knowledge
that my breasts would produce milk,
and my blood still flows regularly
from the hidden mother zone.

I bow to this wise old woman
who is coming,
slowly and surely down this road,
and she is no more a stranger to me
than the face I see in the mirror
in the wavy light of dawn.

Glad Wilderness

Excitement builds on the edge of the world
where I saw the Northern Lights for the first time
and I was afraid to admit my fear—all the way
out here in the strange wilderness of Northern Maine.
"Where are ya from?"
"Away—from away" down south in Dixie—look away.
Yeah. I had to draw the curtains and pretend
I was in another place for a while—

the way I closed myself up to the multitude of lights in New York
City in that hotel with the big windows—
Park Central in December—packed.
Educational conferences were the order of the day, but the lions
at the public library were something we all wanted to see—
a family thing to take our minds away from ground zero
and numbness at the bone. We took pictures there
as night began to overtake
the stairs
leading up
to the massive doors
with Christmas inside: books
wrapped in leather with fine leaves and gold trim—
stuff of dreams to remember. And to think: me, here,
when my daddy and mama, who brought me and seven others
into this world, in South Carolina, couldn't even read and
understand a whole book to save their lives—not even a book
from the Holy Bible. The kids and I lingered over a crack
developing in the right lion, rubbing our cold, gloveless fingers
over its back, not wanting to leave, tremendously saddened
that this fine beast would eventually be torn apart.

"What brings ya up here?"
"Education." Yeah.
We were pulled up by words on the page
and a brand new tenure track job at a university.

"My husband is an Assistant Professor of English."
Morning comes early and night falls swiftly here.
The birds are flocking earlier and that means a harsh winter.
I've got to learn to read the signs for myself
and prepare for weather of a sort I've never known.

> *"The wilderness and the parched land shall be glad*
> *And the desert shall rejoice and blossom as the rose.*
> *It shall blossom abundantly and rejoice,*
> *Even with joy and singing."*
>
> Isaiah 35:1-9

Trio In Blue

1. Triolet on a Cabin in the Woods that Could Have Been

I found out Grandma Reid's house and all the land was sold
when someone up from Florida had paid a right smart sum of money.
I told Mama that I could have bought it if she'd only told
me before Grandma Reid's house and all the land was sold.
She said, "You wairen't here and I never would've knowed
you even wanted it. What would you have done with it, Honey?"
I found out Grandma Reid's house and all the land was sold
when someone up from Florida had paid a right smart sum of money.

2. Triolet on a Choice Color for a Porch Ceiling

Ha'nt Blue ain't just blue; it's blue and grey.
I've seen several shades and there's no doubt.
It's like the sky of a foggy mountain day.
Ha'nt Blue ain't just blue; it's blue and grey.
Sure, it is said to keep old hags away,
while evil spirits and their like stay out.
Ha'nt Blue aint just blue; it's blue and grey.
I've seen several shades and there's no doubt.

3. Triolet on a Line from Our Carpenter

"Angles are hard to figure no matter what..."
He tells me in the slanting end of summer light.
Not much to show for a whole day of work.
Angles are hard to figure no matter what
corners we've cut, saving some, losing a lot.
But I trust this man to know what's right.
Angles are hard to figure, no matter what
he tells me in the slanting end of summer light.

Passing Phrases On Porch Construction

"It's really coming along." "Your porch looks great!"
We hear people say, in passing, as we wait.
"Everyone is going to want a porch like that!"
"Why did you extend it out so much on each end?"
"It makes the house look larger and less square."

We hear people say. "It is taking a long time."
"It's worth the wait!" "Tom's doing stellar work."
"That's not a do-it-yourself job! Not that one there."
"Blue ceilings really do look good, don't they?
I may do that to mine." We hear people say.

"You'll see people doing this to theirs."
"You'll have started up a new trend here."
"I'll put away for a new porch now myself."
"It's almost finished now!" "Your porch looks great!"
We hear people say, in passing, as we wait.

Sui Generis

The realtor said: "What we have here is a one-of-a kind place."
After looking at several houses on the market
we settled on this one just for its location:
within walking distance of the kids' schools
and our jobs at the university—and for the view
of a hill I later found out was called Charette.

The hill has a unique apple tree called the Charette
or Donut Apple, for slices are said to resemble donuts.
The seeds must have come to this place more than 200 years ago,
but the parentage of the only known mature tree is unknown.
It was the view of this hill that helped me find comfort here,
so far away from my own Southern Appalachian hills.

Yes, I agree that "what we have here is a one-of-a kind place."
Our old re-built house has withstood countless snows,
basement floods, roof leaks, frozen pipes and thaws.
We've made some improvements: put on a new roof,
and sealed up the basement windows. Now, we're adding
an extended porch with dormers and a ha'nt blue ceiling.

The porch seems to connect us with a busy community.
Comments on the construction could probably fill up a tome,
and people often have stories to tell about the old place
as it was known before we bought it, or about their own.
People stop by, tell their tales and give me words for poems.
I go in, look out on a hill away from here, feeling not always alone.

About the Author

Geraldine Cannon holds an M.F.A. in Creative Writing—Poetry from the University of Arkansas, at Fayetteville. Cannon has won the John Ciardi Award, the Kenneth Patchen Award, and the Raymond L. Barnes Award for Excellence in Poetry.

Cannon, who grew up in the foothills of the Appalachian Mountains, in the rural town of Salem, South Carolina, now resides with her husband and two children at the other end of the mountain range in the beautiful, rural town of Fort Kent, Maine. She enjoys teaching various types of writing and literature courses as an Assistant Professor of English and Creative Writing for the University of Maine at Fort Kent.

www.ingramcontent.com/pod-product-compliance
Lightning Source LLC
Chambersburg PA
CBHW071028080526
44587CB00015B/2538